THE CARTOGRAPHER OF CRUMPLED MAPS

CRIMINAL JUSTICE :: PASTORAL

poems by

Jonathan Andrew Pérez

Finishing Line Press
Georgetown, Kentucky

THE CARTOGRAPHER OF CRUMPLED MAPS

CRIMINAL JUSTICE :: PASTORAL

DEDICATED TO THOSE WHO STRUGGLE TO ACHIEVE
JUSTICE, AND THE FIGHT

"The measure of a country's greatness is its ability to retain compassion in a time of crisis"
-U.S. Supreme Court Justice, Thurgood Marshall

"Our courts and juries aren't impartial arbiters—they exist inside society, not outside of it—and they can only provide as much justice as society is willing to give."
-Jamelle Bouie, on the grand Jury's image of Michael Brown as the "black brute"

[all footnotes from National Audubon Society, The Sibley Guide to Birds, David Allen Sibley 2000 by Alfred A Knopf Books, Chanticleer Press, Inc.]

Copyright © 2020 by Jonathan Andrew Pérez
ISBN 978-1-64662-175-0 First Edition
All rights reserved under International and Pan-American Copyright Conventions.
No part of this book may be reproduced in any manner whatsoever without written permission from the publisher, except in the case of brief quotations embodied in critical articles and reviews.

ACKNOWLEDGMENTS

A great debt of gratitude is owed to the editors of the following publications where these poems first appeared, often in earlier versions:

Split Lip Magazine: "Choose Your Own Adventure: Reparation as Fable"
Winner of the Split Lip Magazine prize for 2020, judged by Chen Chen
POETRY Magazine: "Bobolinks as a Flock of Signifiers"
The River Heron Review: "Beasts of the American Wilderness"
Dovecote: "Reparation, or the Cartographer of the Godfather of Soul"
Inklette: "Fugitive Acts"
The Bookends Review: "Gulf Fritillary: Agraulis Vanillae"
The Rumble Fish Quarterly: "The Northern Waterthrush"
Muse/ A Journal: "A Dark Etymology: Eastern Meadowlark"
Rise Up Review: "The Multiverse"
Quiddity: "Gospel"
Hiram: "Vignette, 1992"
BARNHOUSE: "Incantation: James Brown"
Projector Magazine: "Pancho Villa by James Dean" "The Varied Thrush"
Crack the Spine: "Indiana Jones' Bathtub"
Cathexis Northwest Press: "Legal Fiction" "Delorean State Prison" "From The Waban Series"
Abstract Magazine: Contemporary Expressions: "Upon Discovering a Floating Corpse at the Rio"
The Worcester Review: "White Supremacy Pamphlet, Coopers Hawk"
The Tulane Review: "The Crown of Leaves: Highway Beautification Act"
The Chicago Quarterly Review: "American Woodcock in the Fog" "The Evening Grosbeak"
The Piltdown Review: "Long Eared Owl: Refuse Container Outside the Metropolitan Museum" "Voodoo Dodo" "Out of Habit" "On a Folksy Painting of Kids Throwing Die, Harlem" "Squirrel Resurrection"
Cape Cod Poetry Review: "Great Blue Heron: The Moon Is a Blood Moon"

Publisher: Leah Maines
Editor: Christen Kincaid
Cover Art: Jonathan Andrew Pérez
Author Photo: Jonathan Andrew Pérez
Cover Design: Elizabeth Maines McCleavy

Printed in the USA on acid-free paper.
Order online: www.finishinglinepress.com
also available on amazon.com

Author inquiries and mail orders:
Finishing Line Press
P. O. Box 1626
Georgetown, Kentucky 40324
U. S. A.

Table of Contents

REPARATION, OR THE CARTOGRAPHER OF THE
GODFATHER OF SOUL 1
CHOOSE YOUR OWN ADVENTURE: REPARATION
AS FABLE 2
THESE SIGNIFIERS AS A FLOCK OF BOBOLINKS 3
THE JUSTICE ELEGY: JOHN DOE 4
KILLDEER 5
FUGITIVE ACTS 6
LAKE OF FIRE, FAR FROM HERE 7
UPON DISCOVERING A FLOATING CORPSE[SHAWL] IN
THE RIO 8
ALIEN IMPORTS 9
MULTIVERSE 4 10
GREAT BLUE HERON: THE MOON IS A BLOOD MOON 11
VIGNETTE 1992 12
A DARK ETYMOLOGY: EASTERN MEADOWLARK 13
DELOREAN STATE PENITENTIARY 14
INDIANA JONES' BATHTUB 15
PANCHOS IN THE DESERTS IN MEXICO 16
GULF FRITILLARY: AGRAULIS VANILLAE 17
HIGHWAY BEAUTIFICATION ACT 18
WHITE SUPREMACY PAMPHLET LONG ISLAND, FALL 1964 20
BARN OWL: BURN BARN, BURN 21
THE NORTHERN WATERTHRUSH 23
WOODCOCK IN THE FOG 24
SQUIRREL RESURRECTION 25
THE DEPORTABLE 26
THE EVENING GROSBEAK 27
OSPREY: THE LAKE 28
ON A FOLKSY COLLAGE OF CHILDREN THROWING DIE,
HARLEM 29
PASSERINES OF DUSK 30
ORDER TO UNSEAL THE PAST: 31

REPARATION, OR THE CARTOGRAPHER OF THE GODFATHER OF SOUL

> Missing Witness: (n. phrase): the expectation by a jury of one's peers that your existence is yours to keep, that you are a witness to salvageable testimony
>
> Posse Comitatus: a fee of $10 a U.S. Marshall can impose for a citizen who aided a fugitive during the 1850 Fugitive Slave Act

i.

Missing witness Charge!   dusk is rapidly falling.
A jury of one's peers   has gone extinct.

Men circled around him   glaring justification.
you cannot trust hearsay.   You cannot unblind
an unsalvageable thing.

It is like it is—*chant, chant,*
the spitting of tobacco juice.
The encore, the clean muscle,   where the brightest
cannot reach.   You were there,

brother from another mother.   Tremendous stings,
like killer bees searching with a flashlight
on wrinkled oak trees,   for shadow-dance,

in spite of the brightness   they cannot reach,
the negative inference   swelling collective testimony.

ii.

Charge! Dusk is rapidly falling, encore!
"Deep River" diametrically   mapping bread-crumb crime scene.
where dim, blisters   on a neck are an exoneration.

Centuries later: silk fine suit, Good Gawdy
on television   we watched Soul thrive visibly
in spite of huge damned bodies, revelation toured crime scene circuity.

The register spits out   10 bucks back (unidentified accounting);
the nation seismically   opens, layer upon layer, titanic crust
fractures: a cake-cream unfurling,

this leitmotif of reparation.

CHOOSE YOUR OWN ADVENTURE: REPARATION AS FABLE

> *1955: Activist Lamar Smith was murdered and remained unsolved after 30 white witnesses did not come forward; no conviction. This was the same year Emmett Till and George W. Lee were killed.*

Fable, lime slugs and mango peepers, hail, under the purple verbena,
    Charge, undertaker, full moon, a version of America cross-hatched,

Two fables, transmogrification and head-in-the-sand, you, choose your own adventure.
    Rush in to fill the gaps; suddenly broad with uncertainty, choose your own witness,

Recognize the moral currency, one-by-one, the other obscured by arrest.
    Above you, a lavender pillow, a scrub grey hairstreak munches early morning dew.

The cold case closed, a body of evidence, an unnatural mailman serves papers anew.
    Moss-infused, turn to page 86! this blood-hound on the stained trail, you repeat a reparation.

    Like deep wounds in the form of indictments sprouted, guilt, an early creek of butterfly sails.
It ribs you, what once was, a pageant to sympathy, a posthumous letter, so.
    Dignity

You, arbiter of your intrinsic red-lined scales, justice, what speckled the sun,
    They found Lamar Smiths body, by the lake where bromeliads bashed.

Who spreads its petals, unrests, she loved me, she loved me not,
    Mother Earth's chrysalis first born, out the garden, wanders the hollows and hails.

Cry hails, cry hails, cry, hails, until it can be heard even with no human breaths.

THESE SIGNIFIERS AS A FLOCK OF BOBOLINKS

       This neighborhood map thrives on rising sentences
arbitrary *Icterid* with signified arms; Ventriloquist!
       shook-throated, a rock-hard reed-lance thorn by the landfill—
a bird almost-mistook-for erasure shared in a thin migration,
       like marauding packs of boys who fight or make out, discover song,
  hinge:
on the talk or sheen of feeling, grass-rooted as if contra-the wind enough to
  prevent erasure?
       Its moat of fear, reinvented burps, throbbing streetlamp burst on the fritz,
the self-appointed-like throat, chewed on ambition, held choked as a corn-flavored
  chip,

fed and left to dust the milk of the park, where seaward, another earth throws
  shade:
       the moon, almost, or a hurricane, we dawn and we signify our own
  sentences'
justice, justice, built on migration from conjugations the winds once institutionally
  appointed:
       at last—this hurricane!

THE JUSTICE ELEGY: JOHN DOE

> *Chicago v. Morales: A local ordinance, Chicago's Gang Congregation Ordinance to prohibit "criminal street gangs" from loitering in public places. The Supreme court found that such loitering laws, better known as Broken Windows Theory, violated the Due Process Clause of the Constitution.*

Broken Windows Theory: a thing of a fractured mind, a frontier
      for defiant squatters—seeking the light, broken by windows,
stumbling in unbridled night; John Doe stipulated to lamentation
      near a car parked, by a government-owned landmark sign.

Abolitionist place, for tourists to take photos, folksy-like-radiant
      boardwalk out-light, stutter, where none belonged, this daydream
without origin. A stray cat played on a plain curbside, in cooler rooms of hell,
      of the Bowery and nine times bet its Wheel of Fortune.

Spectral shadow, John Doe. There is a drumming in the marsh.
      We do not ever leave, we are locked in the wind, together
standard placeholders for unidentified, to be rebroadcast, closer to the edge
      of discovery, to swim, illustrious, out in foam-green esplanade scarfed-

bodies unidentified on the cold slab of the city morgue,
      on the side of the congregants, swollen, reproachable, unfounded charges,
long past the anonymous universe that birthed them in.

KILLDEER

1935 Thomas A. Dorsey invents Take My Hand Precious Lord

There was peace in this valley. White-black winged plovers
fake injury on hot gravel. These large Killdeer,
incandescent, jig on Lake Michigan. August heat,
bathe and speakeasy in sunlight. Sidewalk honey
drip and sing, hullabaloo, despite a Great Depression.

There, the Baptist Convention, cars raced overhead
on the northside. *I am tired and I am alone.* Lead me, let me
stand, I am weak. Killdeers fake winged injury.
Folky trumpet blow, croon, cream, rook, a great spiral
of buzzard in the tempest: Coltrane *Live in Japan*.

Blood-hot boys eye white dresses, cool, meet in Cadillacs.
Rough engine roar parking lot, bass beat, Killdeer
killy killy killy, rattle the concrete valley. Lampshade bright
underbelly of Chicago at night, French, Louisiana, euro-
flare, she met who? where? He is slim, she glistens in birthing sin.

Stand by me, Lord do take my precious hand. The Blind Boys
of Alabama, thunder blossoms like Lilac meadows, hiding
stray cats in alleyway cracks, over the Sears Tower.
Billowed Gospel. Wind from white buildings.
By the Packinghouse, workers watch late shift—

another fella, another time, she walked alone.
Shorebirds rise. The concrete gave a circumspect Amen.

FUGITIVE ACTS

Shadroch Minkins walked out federal prison.

I.
Hear, beneath the dearth of sky.
Hear, the buried dead in a seated posture.
     "follow the drinking gourd!
follow the drinking gourd!"

Hear, an empty search warrant to the soul.
A hand, quaint, flirted a bone heap, in wooded patrol.
    Dim and dark runs, from Alabama
    up the Tombigbee only runs
cold in the woodcutter's veins;

not among black— what stalks in silence
          against the black skies
in cover of mother sky. Let lanterns, enter-
    let petals fly—regard, the   light
    now let me fly, now let me fly.

II.
Search the deepest hollow,   the light is in the east
    fill a pattern transformed,
    the song of the promised land.

    Land in the common lilies, among shadows
    Property-less breath, heart, sweat, nose.

There were lions in the way, *I don't expect to stay much longer—despite,*
this ancient game of go.

          III
The canary in the coal-mine,
my drum fell where the dead
turned pale-faced, no turmoil,
nor sweat nor tears nor sweat,
a sympathizer in the stocks
a cabin that offers exigency plans.
Foaming dogs tear   lyrics, by strict lines of undergrowth.

Hear, the city where once, children, dreamt of life,
where Dad happened   to pass an angel.
Hear, it fall from the sky.

This extradition has no space to hold:
A democracy like instinct   opens a shuttered eye.

LAKE OF FIRE, FAR FROM HERE

> *"But for the cowardly and unbelieving and abominable and murders and immoral persons and sorcerers and idola-ters and all liars, their part will be in the lake that burns with fire and brimstone, which is the second death."* —Revelation 21:8

At La Purisima Concepcion Mission,
I imagined a wall of fire,
then broke through it. Out on the Western
Wall, Texans, Californians smelt autumn red-ridge bluegrass
around the lone star pontoon. San Francisco de los Neches
and a family used to live here. A family who owned this
shelter lived down the shores. The Colorado river
bastion - has tides the modern world
has not seen: nomadic, oracular
Indigenous People, Tonkawa, drove
eternal cattle off imagined cliffs. San Jose de los Nazonis
Apache then French ransacked the family who made Heaven out of the modern world,
sky a memorial to them, who hollered distant rage
near the bat lookout, like a light
for the heated signals of planes.
An air traffic controller against settlers up there sought
shelter away from here. The thunder
clap is a spoof on their folkloric
Nature, outspread abyss permanent
settlements, soupy bottom less, or
a mirage of a convenience store with
drifters and Tall Boys. We contain
embers of the old families, Mexican
immigrants and Spanish friar royalty.

Some stampeded like Buffalo off
the shorn cliff, in penal fire, made it
across the lake of understanding where
all is perennially torture and sulphur, where
only the dead souls worship, burned
away by alcohol and fear.

Near the arborist pupils of the river, howls
of Comanche—melted skinny figures
dance, ghosts or laughing otherworldly
stick figures, seek refuge in not being
from here, far, far, from now, darkness visible now.

UPON DISCOVERING A FLOATING CORPSE[SHAWL] IN THE RIO

Families on the *Rio Grande* nestle in solitary ponds, tide low,
bob-huts against the wind. Search in mud, wet up to the

exposed fiddler crabs (*pre-columbian* before Spanish Conquistadores
they travel displaced but Puebla); they sat in families

along corner-marshes, pursuing the predicament of shuttle-liminal
footsteps & appeasing notions of the water table. ~~One floating corpse.~~[Shawl]

They return—the inventory of survival mechanisms, a cousin prays to
Catarina de San Juan.
An aunt's Sari embroidered with nobility of horsemanship and brute strength.

Fishing was necessary for survival, tools, plants into beds were in reunion
with utilitarianism, agriculture and ranching. The far-off guttural sounds

that alert the coast guard, the backwoods Ranger, sinking into notebooks with statistics,
that elaborate that ~~body's~~ [shawl's] *botoneria*, silver buttons waiting, praying,
and rebirthing life to risk death.

ALIEN IMPORTS

Big brother burned their decks,
campaigned against their unseen feelers.
Despite our insensitive instruments
they survived their genocide.

Millions & millions
—bloom & blossom—un-failed.
They, hungry for ascending mosaics
spill the dew & explode in a million flints.

The old and shamanic ones lived out
the remainder of their years in holes-in-the-wall.
Until one escaped on a pier, with the quahog,
& overtook the mainsail.

So began the start of civilization.

MULTIVERSE 4

> *Gun Control: (phrase) the idea that the world of Man and Will can overcome Divine Intervention*

It was suggested that a comet made a hole
In the chest of beauty, the final bullet gloom and ray slit,
Elongated streams in the river like processions of the dead,
The endangered after this, had no dominion in the solar system.

The motionless balm held intercourse with a wide dominion.
An elliptical voice from the icy bank took on less than a coherent second;
Melodious, golden, questioning all the canvas: duck, tide, sheen, glimmer,
For large-mannered reasoning to explain away with vigor. Dislodge.

> The difference between the levels in the multiverse correspond to where
> Your doppelgangers reside.
> Level III is three-dimensional space, while another quantum branch may be infinite
> dimensional.

To dislodge the billions their polymer tips, crept in.
From fields, trees, arms, legs, skulls
Bits to bite into, and to comb the stream.
To bid farewell: no more buckshot, pinpoint accuracy, Community Patrol Officers.
In this world, the lost children will cheer each other on,
At the middle school production
And their children's children will not be molded by fear.

GREAT BLUE HERON: THE MOON IS A BLOOD MOON

Ode to a body named Washington, in Waco, Texas, May 15, 1916

I.

By the County Court, a Great Blue Heron[1],
Stalks the Texas Tall Grass, Waco.
The moon is a blood moon.

The embers of the event, be still,
Spectators howl, fire, Waco wetlands
on the outskirts of the city.

II.

Cattail and waterlily,
emblematic of a missing feature.
An oxygenated flint mistook the shiver of fire sheen for life.

It is I who had been left out in a dry heap,
It is I one by one from jury, who cannot convict.
It is I who you will see that this crack will become a more serious fissure.

III.

This torment of lunar encroachment, ghosts
or frogs croak in millions of streams of starry fields.
All is buried beneath the landscape of nolo contendere.

The Heron sucked out snails like venom
And its materiality disappeared in the sun and birch
In its place, the relief of a thundering patch of lake and grass.

---

[1] *Ardea herodias: L. 46" ws: 72" Largest and heaviest heron is one of the most vocal, calling frequently in flight. Large, sturdy; heavy bill. White morph resembles Great Egret. Flight call a very deep, hoarse trumpeting fraaahnk, or braak.*

VIGNETTE 1992

Eclipsed: Western Logic, Arithmetic that universe they used to read Miranda rights:
You have the right to remain silent, anything you say or do will be used against you.

Even if you are silent, backed up to 1992 Rodney King blacked & blued
therefore, hence, ergo the L.A. night, proud fires spelled rights in fumes & rose anew.

first-order predicate logic: schools, EBT, behavioral therapy, Planet, nothing was used against you.
proof-theory stolen body like a clank or holler right structurally in The Marcus Garvey Houses:

Uncle Diego opened the gate for los gatos again. We watched, 1992, tv news.
Strict mathematics, pure deduction, what represented burning bushes & spoke of imagination,

my brother spray painted UFOs, and a feminine script on the Orange Line Station. This wasn't our world to rebuild, our *"if I say this, then it must be this"* commuted our sentences.

A DARK ETYMOLOGY: EASTERN MEADOWLARK

The meadowlark[2] careens a cracked marsh,
historical dogwood stands stark incanting
the alarms of pollution,
we once spelled "the world is on fire," but held, a demiurge.

Tan-brown boys are terrified by winds bigger than men.
outside, alone, he kicks a stone, loosened
by Hurricane Sandy,
where, near Avenue U, grandpa
used to roll cigars on Marine Salt Marsh, before.

The apocalyptic phragmites
find an expressway,
  No men thwart angels,
only the meadowlark stands in, a hypothesis for the fact we sinned.

Elders once envisioned stumbling creatures,
descending Eden,
  housing on outskirts of saltwater-cities,
  the neon from water treatment plant—
Wings blackened the dripping sun & attested
to make a tired argument for ascetism.

---

[2] *Sturnella magna L. 9.5" ws: 14" heavy-bodied, short-tailed, and long-billed. Obvious white outer tail feathers. Song of simple, clear, slurred whistles seeeooaaa seeeadoo with many variations. Flight call a thin, rising veet or rrink.*

DELOREAN STATE PENITENTIARY

A few hundred feet from his resurrection,
DeLorean rolls up to the prison
inmate No. 5400 has no harbor of
absolution but a time exertion push to a Future past—

Do, at midnight, 1.21 gigawatts
Ride out
no savior to ream
erased mysteriously
from the State Penalty Review Commission final decision.

He sits in the tent
Little knowledge of a doc's bullet proof vest
the final Sunday flying out choppy waters.

Thinks of daddy and examines
spring peepers, and nabs a worm for feeder,
return to the future—

kiss mama, say you're sorry to miss it

For Monday morning's fishing trip
hover craft board, you'll utter
all the things to pops, never did say
no record of it, no Country, nor history can name it: break out.

INDIANA JONES' BATHTUB

Ethnographic Indiana Jones: I am no ancient statue;
a differentiated genetic instruments; which no blow-dart gun can stun.

Collector, conservator
A floating talisman   race the primal diet
Is your error
You are not my captor
no Western trawling ships
extend upward and down

unwound ropes, a childish thing, burned our name in the museum
With little to preserve but all to capture.

We live past extinction and reinvent our heritage

like a wild hyena.

PANCHOS IN THE DESERTS IN MEXICO

Point of no return: (n.) the theory of no more second chances, loss of a mythic savior

Ocotillo bloom once a year in post-apocalyptic thunder dome biome,
Save that one night, it wasn't too dry,
uttered these dying words;
A single *Federale* turned his head the other way—

Pancho, jettied and hurtled
the Great Basin, like Mad Max,
between depression and the slope of testy machismo
brigadier keep in store a life, not grow old,

a lump in a final sand-filled throat, dystopic larynx speak truth,
a vulture bit the flapping skin bandit
left his buckle, a long pistol,
the rest slipped away

in the cacti constitution
for child's rhymes on a squalid backroad wishing
they could ride a steed named Valor to a Hollywood sunset
ream out the division between this world

and the roaring firetip of eternally-sentenced Idealists.

GULF FRITILLARY: AGRAULIS VANILLAE

A bottle and Styrofoam container against the passionflowers
the silver-streaked scrub hopper, took to the chestnut light:

what we resist, breathlessly we visit in our sleep
like the Fritillary[3] among the bog, drawn from long nectar pints:

when I was born, I stood origin-less like the hunger along the Rio Grande.
Among the stray flight on brush stalk, a selective mutism

reticulated, variegated, an artifact that crossed from Mexico
from Sonoran folkloric sustenance, and in the gulf, chestnut sunlight,

stamped out an unseen pirouette, breathless, like a Cordera
sung to later generations struggling to resist, inherited

on a day-laborer's rucksack, Regal Fritillaries disappeared from the East
in the late 1970s; now a Calvary belts out in strands along abandoned
Forts

near dried-cracked Pastures: the softest part of a rose preexisted
the emerging violets in their fragility last forever:

no one noticed, not even in a eulogy, when the last one dropped.

---

[3] *Agraulis Vanillae. This bright lively butterfly frequent open, scrubby habitats. Gulf Frittalry was named (or misnamed) on the basis of its appearance more than its ancestry. They belong to a group of "straight line migrants." Prefers open, scrubby habitats. Maypops. Passionflower.*

17

HIGHWAY BEAUTIFICATION ACT

> "Beauty Belongs to All The People"—
> President Lyndon & Lady Bird Johnson
> Highway Beautification Act, 1965

Shady: (v.) beyond logic, bias of older, established trees

i.
Trucks pass, the first of that species, gouged air,
a city gullet shivers the rest of those who do not flee.

Maple, Ginko Biloba: leaves pick up the swell. With God's help I am able.
To the elongated crumpled edges between Exit 9-a and Jones Beach Loopway

spotty, a stroke in the blanket of legislation, the whiff of smog.
Vagrants drop between goldenrod in temporary puddles.

The black-throated green warbler[4] scratchy— shadowless, overcast landscape
a painter's tree siphons the continual breeze, meadow from brook,

ii.
darting zees in private ziplines that copter from Fire Island, to vacationland,
past erased islands, setting the bright compass to well past Rikers.

Joints are joisted, we do not live in passing, the slow flapping of wings,
By the exit sign, a faint clammy day, we stay and small rarities, linger.

The bud has pushed into the crown and flittering gnatcatchers pillow the clean white,
born into a chrysalis of leaves beneath a world of sky;

in between, shaded flowers are naked, protected in the womb of sun.
This chance for insects they cherished the opportunity

having undaunted access won, and without the return of winter
the basket of leaves will catch the other ones.

---

[4] *Dendroica virens: L. 5" ws: 7.75" Olive auriculars, bright green back, and yellow wash across vent distinctive. Song a series of short, level buzzes; two commonly heard patterns: a rather fast zee zee zee zee zo zeet and a more relaxed zooooo zee zo zo zeet; some Townsend's songs similar.*

iii.

Brittled by the elements: air, sea, rain, an Exodus crackled by acorns, wicked like shell-horns, which crept along at mercy, elemental, pandered their impartial light.

When I am alone, I fight, the flittering that catapults me out, into levity. But I am not a leaf falling. I am not a seed. I have no made my back into the tree.

I'm from way out in shade.
By the shimmy of injustice – jumping between shadows for eternity.

WHITE SUPREMACY PAMPHLET LONG ISLAND, FALL 1964

The State's offer, after, affected your immigration status
while on parole. You just got work, feet up, & pretend cruelty

killed your dreams, but the intellect controls.
Franz Fanon, resist, Baraka beard, down to your chest, thick rims bluesily.

A Farmingdale College major in theater: tempered
from your garage, blasted *Elton John, Philadelphia Freedom.*

Anonymous cherub from a Walmart sale, left on the porch,
blotched, to scare you, left outside like a Seventh Day

Adventist pamphlet, beneath a cracked crib, an omen
to Christmas, overblown. A Cooper's Hawk swooped,

cameras covered in cobwebs. The orange scent
from candle emanated down the tree-lined stillness

*Day laborers not welcome here: no speaky English,
no job, not your Land*

in the distilled distance. Why start to roam?
A citizen's safety patrol, an homage to the winter—

frozen bark clung to community, dark, skeptical
& resilient, but still in existence, despite blowing leaves.

*Who called the police on the neighbors—
who refused to be interviewed by the long skein*

*of stark uniform voices, at 3am? Who shattered your leaves
& left a picture bruised by the idea of intruder?*

The tea kettle blasted, years later, blue-gray rug,
large Oak in Huntington, not-assimilated family outside,

smoking long drawls on cigars, cigarillo, &
dipping white cigarettes. In the distance

flocks of American Pipits scrambled from the Hawk,
searched barren forests among the liminal suburban woods,

      where all was historically undernourished.

BARN OWL: BURN BARN, BURN

Barn (n.): that thing that looks like a house, but has high vaunted ceilings

My father used to say,
Don't own a little nest-infested barn.

Don't sit all day, writing spiritual poems,
like a Barn Owl[5], or a bleached Ghost.

Until the barn burns, ambiguous as a lung.
Hoot while the smoke doesn't fill your lungs.

Burn (v.): translate without use of a translator, transfiguring

Wake before dawn. Then you go to sleep.
Migrate in the afternoon. Read Borges, Neruda,

mostly maybe *Los Cantos* de Lorca, we migrate
when we know that fire is just oxygen cast as performance.

Burn Bar (n.): phrase meaning to leave, take and run

Owls sleep during the waking hours.
I do not speak Spanish, but I am Spanish.

I maintain the right to be forgotten.
At twilight I own my own despondency.

Reticence: A danceable feast: fiestas, carnivals, gentleness, communities, without smoldering, in the garden of the untimely.

The dead do not sleep. The dead are late-comers.
They watch in corners of barns, cut-off.

Burn (v.): to lose and begin without I.D.

In me sits a mud jar of empathy:
For those who lived.

---

[5] *Tyto Alba: L.16" ws: 42" hunts mainly on the wing at night, patrolling open areas in search of rodents. Broad but fairly pointed wings, large head, long legs; pale tawny and white plumage and heart-shaped face distinctive. Common call year-round simply a long hissing shriek cssssssshhhH. Female call averages softer than male and juvenile averages less hoarse, but overall little variation.*

The opposite of fuel is entropy.
There is no justice in fourth-generations.

The opposite of hate, the sharp shrill of love,
belong a burning pledge, a folk song of death.

After his divorce, my father returned his books
to the library of lost borrowing cards.

He returned His-Panic, and took a terrible leap
across the country, from me left no history.

THE NORTHERN WATERTHRUSH

The Magician of Justice
walked all night in circles.
What rots inside of him—streams of blue darners
dance spun
felt like magic, or, baptized
formless schools below,
where laced wings in waterlogged lances
mark the sign of tight abdomens.

The magician hatched another plan,
one that waxes and wanes
on brown and black solvent
enjoins shed skin, marks lithe play, least distraught
in pools, lets dissipate the dregs of the river's debt.

The Northern Waterthrush[6]
in motion with the migratory rush
runs but rarely finds a spot.
One still figures in rapid sprout
a quicksand of weaponized flight,
spins around the center, or, is perfect
silvery stirring calm.

Nothing will hurt us.
We are invincible.
Soon another will rise rapidly
from what batch calcified and merged
with saltier scrawls below.

The magician of justice read
the fates of randomness,
as the Oracle of Delphi,
captured an imprisoned net
of spawning growth

and spat out, foresaw, letting some go
and grow from puerile worms
to glowing rays and shadows
into pure crossfire.

---

[6] *Seiurus noveboracensis*: L. 6" ws: 9.5" *Both waterthrushes are rather long-bodied, with narrow heads, short tails, and long legs. Song of loud emphatic, clear chirping notes generally falling in pitch and accelerating; loosely paired or tripled, with little variation. Flight call a buzzy, high, slightly rising zzip.*

WOODCOCK IN THE FOG

I saw an old man, or a Woodcock[7],
waiting out the fog, turns his will
over, untangling thick fishnets
with the hourly tide.
The Sardine Factory
behind him,
the cold vast bay,
the harbor swirled in
saltwater ponds,
calm, composed,
the fallow sea meant
little to him, moral
inventory, as the
fleet that hauled
in buoys, dead seals,
and left tread marks
on the way
to further shoals.

Now the splinters
of the sky, now
the December muse
offers her wool skirt
in retribution for
the wait, one drift-
wood pile iced
with change, fearless
and the ice plants
that with tendons
stretch beneath
the swing-set that
creaking bahk bahk
sounds as if there were
someone to catch.

---

[7] *(Scolopax minor): L. 11" ws: 18" American Woodcock if found in damp, brushy, woods, displaying birds choose grassy or brushy fields nearby. Plump with long bill; large head; broad rounded wings; short legs. Solitary and secretive with cryptic pattern, unlike any other shorebird. Flight call absent. Wings produce a high twittering on takeoff and when making sharp turns in flight; higher-pitched and clearer than Mourning Dove.*

SQUIRREL RESURRECTION

Oakland squirrel on the street—RIP:
its language was like Coleridge's albatross
that spoke through the neck of a Hanged Man
or an Emperor, a phrase dashed on a Tarot Card.
Redemption—the body of the squirrel enshrined
like a statue surfaced on the frozen-divine glossed
concrete street lake, swept by sweepers in a dusky city park,
there, first letter last initial, an unnamed splotch of soul
gone by the end of season's yellow washing.

THE DEPORTABLE

> *"Speak, Memory—of the cunning hero, the wanderer, blown off course time and again"* —Homer, *The Odyssey Book I*
>
> *"And that god snuffed out their day of return."* —Homer, *The Odyssey Book I*

Solstice- vagrant life, inherit language, death, fugitive symbolism
He must not see the guilt, hung by necks of Emperors, or keep stealing.
Tarot reading blood & bones –a bondsman's schism
Douglass to England, a splotchy Jesus bankrupt our surety needing,
Poor am I now green worms & contraband follow my future sleeping;
A father, foretold, before bed, child rhymes of seceding, West Indies-bred.
An angel fell moonward loose of bondsmen, sun rise with none weeping.
1846 to 1966, this deportable *translation*: I am I, not be charged meaning instead.

Deportable bodies twitch in heaven, stoops lit extricate unsung army of monks
Ad hoc committee of angels of injustice, swift above Oakland, send safety nets:
Chant terror sing, police, felled by Icarus-like wings bend wax funk.
Our fury *shivers* our backs, sends us back by railroad years outside walls to sweat.
American stock market, invest less in the coroner's candlelight vigil bet—
Emancipate policy men who earn just to be just—quiet now bullet-box rough
Come ladies and Gentlemen, all bets on red—I am he who fell centuries bereft
A birth rite place is there, deported, flesh of my flesh extradited American handcuff.

He who knows himself well shall humble in His presence,
Spit out, earthquake rumble of the Mexican Revolution, Zapatistas burned
1911 instead, vested in pools blood of my blood, dismissed, taught lessons
Mexican Mermaid, *they say, or chant contemplates*, in canals bad earned
There is a barrio where the Mermaids took conquistadores gravely to stem ferns.
Xochimilco, the whole tide white-black, all billions return wind-myth washed it
There is a barrio not far from an Undiscovered City, and freedom turned
Based on the evidence, admit, the deported acquit and now on thrones exist, upon which no master sits.

THE EVENING GROSBEAK

They found the most beautiful thing, in antiquity
Blew dust off its bright yellow chest, like a gold statue.

The expungement of a record, I was not a latch key kid but due
a fort to return to, not a broken home, made my own
        archaeology through
Violence, rarity, history, ratified by songbirds in the public
        boughs, alone
These parents, gathered food stamps, dove from child services,
        missed the milieu
That bloomed on a windowsill—the fragile thing called when none
        could answer the phone.

The poisoned berry, an uncited statistic, caught the child as she flew
        out of home and rose
Over the play of history: Arkansas national guards blocked grandpa's school,
separate but equal,
From the bottom of the bush, she saw the dark furrowed brow of the
        sky, a show
Condensed in the unsoundable swell, the last Grosbeak[8] braved
        the blank easel
To ask her why the slow atonement is never done, why she is not yet
        a steeple
Rinsed like a throat from which other children sang, a lyric that we are
        all colorful summations
At the end of a long and furious argument about an error: I'm sorry
        for seeming illegal

The Grosbeak waded in the snow, found seed, and buried foot near
        her soul, on the disfigured nation.
The loneliness of the Grosbeak rang in a great choir, through
        the petals

Rode the wind perfectly—with a gust of Grace, as a beast of no nation,
But for the wild rejoice to weave and flitter between images legal
        and illegal
And not cave in but live past erasure & division.

---

[8] *Coccothraustes vespertinus: L. 8" ws: 14" Massive head and bill, short tail, relatively short but pointed wings. White wing-patches always conspicuous. Song apparently a regular repetition of call notes. Call a high, sharp, ringing trill kleerr reminiscent of House Sparrow; in flocks a low, dry rattle or buzz thirr. flight call a high, clear whistled teew not ringing or trilled.*

OSPREY: THE LAKE

All is crystal and
invigorating at the lake.

Two boys in scuba gear
prowl the reflective depths.

The Osprey[9] glides
over the watery outcrops.

A Brown Trout snaps
near the deaf underwater divers.

A raft ferries the last
of the vacationers over to the log cabin.

From the look of it, the weather
will not delay tomorrow.

---

[9] *Pandion haliaetus: L. 23" ws: 63" Long, narrow wings always angled and bowed down; gull-like. Shape and underwing pattern distinctive. Quite vocal; all calls short, shrill whistles tewp, tewp, tewp, teelee, teelee, tewp; commonly single loud, shrill, slightly slurred whistle teeeeaa.*

ON A FOLKSY COLLAGE OF CHILDREN THROWING DIE, HARLEM

Rattle: Looking at the folksy painting,
Black Odyssey, *tap, tap, tap,* kids throw die,
Black street white sky jazz-guitar magic
That stoops cartomancy foretold,
alabaster cloud to banister.

Expectations ravage the experimental shrine,
a Southern Baptism
Dunks the young child, hands up,
and bends moon-ward without a sigh.

Escape the city sweltering
summer law enforcement sweeps.
Throw die like Carolina Wrens[10] rattle
on fragrant white lilies, *Zhwee, zhwee, zhwee.*

Purple socks, long coats and straw hats
on orange hill, mandarin
snake eyes, die: twitch in heaven,
shoot spring flecked grass bumps.

Smoke thirsty souls
catch industry cigar breaks, in staccato nets:
Catch what youth has gambled, return the communal allowance.

I stood upright in the evening,
paint a canvas I knew nothing about
but took on the overwhelming innocence of all things, even life.

It shrouded in peaks of reeds,
Communicated with the unseen, then
Fell to pieces.

---

[10] *Thryothorus ludovicianus: L. 5.5" ws: 7.5" Wrens are mostly small brown, and active but secretive; they creep through vegetation, foraging for insects and fruit, often with their tails raised above their backs, Large-headed, short-billed, and stocky overall with bright reddish-brown plumage. Extremely varied. Song a rolling chant of rich phrases pidaro pidaro pidaro or TWEE pudo TWEE pudo TWEEP and other variations.*

PASSERINES OF DUSK

Rumbling: (v.) the sense of discomfort when that particular sight is migratory, fleeting

The rumbling is the rumbling
Of the shadow of the Gods
Like piano-playing shaped leaves
Or the pitter-patter of rain
That graces the palmetto forest.

It is 4:35pm in Key West
The last passerine, magenta or indigo, a Cerulean Warbler[11]
Streaks across the flagrant ocean sky
And cuts slits right through
The afternoon mint-flavored High Tea.

Passerine: (n.) a migratory bird that braves the skies, flies overnight, a few-time immigrant

The dwarf pines are a diaspora in the scrub,
Neither here nor there,
They are a philosophy all alone
A Mount Olympus in the sweltering heat
To the billions of nearly-visible particles
That could be dirt or sand fleas.

The rumbling is the rumbling
Of the last passerine
Shot out of the shadow of the Gods
While the overside of trees wait
And see what only once
The sea-foam of the littoral
Could muster up the brazenness to see.

The last Cerulean cutting up the sky
Is evidence that everything is changing.

---

[11] *Dendroica cerulea*: L. 4.75" ws: 7.75" Wood Warbler, genus Dendroica, Cerulean nests in tall broadleaf trees near water (e.g. along rivers); very short-tailed, short-legged and stout billed, with very pointed wings. Blue or blue-green upperparts are always distinctive. Song a high musical buzz tzeedl tzeedl tzeedl ti ti ti tzeeeeee, generally three-part each part higher than the preceding one; more musical than parulas with no slurred notes.

ORDER TO UNSEAL THE PAST:

AT A REFUSE CANISTER OUTSIDE THE METROPOLITAN MUSEUM

Raking cracked leaves by the Met Museum.
A paper like an Order for unsealing the past in a canister.
They found your father's father on the roadside.
Here lieth First Man. Let the new ones in.
The street sweeper post-felon cleaner found you.
A Cleric of cracked oak trees, Long Eared Owl.[12]
There ripped dog-eared: the Order, an administered penalty.
We are born, men like me, on the outside looking in.
With no more 2nd chances, the unsanitary removal.
It splashes cupped cracked leaves—C.S. Bishop, 1849,
invented the first street sweeping machine.
This quest from outside, Rembrandt, Renaissance.
The American Tank Company was built on sweat and leaves.
Papers picked from beneath benches.
Those who requested leave without pay, leave.
Newer machines collected smaller particles of debris.
An Order for Unsealing outside the Met.
Your history is that of a choreography, convicted.
Like a brush-stroke of deep verdant oil on a Catalan landscape.
The Long-Eared Owl stared down our pined-up years.

---

[12] *Asio Otus: L.15" ws: 36" hunts mainly on the wing at night, patrolling open areas in search of rodents. Fairly long-winged and slender; wings shorter and broader than Short-eared. Male gives a low, soft hoot wooip about every three seconds. Female call higher and softer sheoof. Alarm (both sexes) variable soft, nasal barks bwah, bwah, bwah.*

Jonathan Andrew Pérez, Esq. has published poetry online and in print in *Prelude, The River Heron Review, Blood Tree Literature, The Write Launch, Meniscus Literary Journal, Rigorous, The Florida Review, Panoply Magazine, The Raw Art Review, Junto Magazine, Blood Tree Literature, Cold Mountain Review, Piltdown Review, Yes, Adelaide Literary Magazine, Mud Season Review, Meat for Tea: the Valley Review, Poached Hair, The Esthetic Apostle, The Tulane Review, Spectrum Journal, The Tiny Journal, Muse/ A Journal, The Bookends Review, The Westchester Review, Metafore, Crack the Spine Quarterly, Silver Needle Press, Projector Magazine, Cape Cod Poetry Review, Rise Up Review, BARNHOUSE, The Chicago Quarterly Review, The Worcester Review, Abstract: Contemporary Expressions, Cathexis Northwest Press, Inklette, Rumblefish Quarterly, Hiram Poetry Review* and *Quiddity* on NPR and *POETRY MAGAZINE*.

Jonathan was selected by Cave Canem in 2018 and 2019 for workshops. He is a 2019 Pushcart Prize in Poetry Nominee. He won Split Lip Press' Poetry Prize for 2019. He is a reader for Rumpus Poetry.

He has a day job as a trial attorney.

www.ingramcontent.com/pod-product-compliance
Lightning Source LLC
LaVergne TN
LVHW041509070426
835507LV00012B/1431